Unless otherwise indicated, all Scriptures quotations are taken from NIV
unless otherwise noted.

THE HOLY BIBLE, NEW INTERNATIONAL VERSION®, NIV®
Copyright © 1973, 1978, 1984, 2011 by Biblica, Inc.™ Used by permission.
All rights reserved worldwide.

www.virgilwoods.com

First Edition: 2015

ISBN-13:9780692555408

Think Like A Fish
2016 Virgil Woods

Think Like A Fish
by dr. virgil woods

Table of Contents

Introduction

I like to fish, but I have never considered myself a real fisherman. I know the basics of fishing, and I have stood on countless shores and in numerous boats trying my hand at catching these seemingly evasive creatures. So when my friend Lenard called and said he was coming to visit me in Iowa and wanted to go fishing, I knew I would need some help. You see, Lenard is a die-hard outdoorsman—and that is probably an understatement. Lenard does not like fishing, he does not love fishing, he *lives* fishing. If Lenard were given the choice of meeting the President of the United States of America or catching large-mouth Bass, well...I would tell the President not to hold his breath.

I knew I needed help to meet Lenard's fishing expectations so I called my brother-in-law Judd. Judd was born and raised in rural Iowa. His high school graduating class had only 14 students and his combined second and third grade class had 8. He was a small-town man, he lived near a good-sized lake, and, like my friend Lenard, he too was a die-hard outdoorsman. I knew Judd would be the perfect tour guide for this trip.

When Lenard and I arrived at Judd's farm, my brother-in-law had the boat ready to go and we decided to fish near his home. It was a beautiful morning and as we trolled into the open area of the lake, we could see other boats getting into position for today's catch.

The day started off slowly, and it wasn't long before I realized just how little I knew about fishing. Lenard and Judd were talking reels and lines and bait and motors and depth finders and using many other terms I had not even heard before. I tried to listen intently, but I may just as well been watching an old Russian play in its original language. I couldn't keep up. These guys were for real.

The first catch always comes as a surprise. Lenard had apparently been trying a few different things and finally found a winning combination. He told me and Judd what he discovered; Judd laughed and said, "Let me try that." Sure enough, it worked. For the next 2 hours, we would catch fish non-stop. I stopped counting at nearly 100 fish. As quick as we could get a baited hook in the water, another one of us was pulling a fish up. It became so ridiculous that other boats tried to ease into our area, assuming our position on the lake had something to do with our success.

After a while, I asked Lenard and Judd why we were having so much success. They talked about the color of the water, the time of day, the particular bait, the flow and direction of water movement across the lake, the type of fish in the area and even the time of year we were fishing. I was amazed and humbled at the same time. The reason for their success was simple. They knew how to think just like a fish. They knew where the fish would be—and even why and when they would be there.

So, what's all of this got to do with churches? I think the same principle applies. If we are called to be fishers of people, shouldn't we truly know the people we are trying to catch—or guide into a relationship with Christ? Shouldn't we know the best time of day to get their attention? Shouldn't we know the right bait to use to even attract them and persuade them to take a closer look at the Christ we offer? What temperature suits the fish in your area best?

I think it's important for leaders of churches to begin to see their churches as outsiders see them, much like fish in a sea. We are trying to attract those fish and draw them into our churches, but we need to begin to see what the fish see, not what we see or want them to see. It can be challenging for people inside of the church to understand how the church's atmosphere is perceived by outsiders. Members have chosen this church for particular reasons and probably love it—or at least love some aspects of the church. But in order to attract those on the outside, both pastors and lay leaders will need to think like fish—see church like the onlookers see it. We will need to speak the same language as the fish we're trying to catch and serve the food they eat as we guide them to our places of worship.

As easy as it may sound initially, seeing the church as fish do is difficult for many believers. Many of us were raised in the church and thus have no idea what life looks like in its absence. We've never been new to a church. Ask yourself a question: when was the first time you went to church? Interesting enough, you probably don't have a date because most church members were born and raised in a church environment.

That's why I think this book will assist churches in one of our main missions—evangelizing.

I pray the messages in this book will not only encourage and also equip you to think more like a fish when viewing your congregation, but will give you the tools needed to nurture a loving and welcomed environment that shares the love and grace of Christ with others and draws them closer to God— even if it draws them closer to another church. The vision is to make sure our churches reflect Christ's nature in all that we do and say.

I've been preaching, teaching, and practicing all of the messages in this book. As a pastor for more than 15 years, I've had the privilege of shepherding churches in a number of contexts, from small rural congregations to large, downtown churches, including the United States and Canada. I also have completed my doctoral studies in congregational development.

This book takes all of the lessons I've learned firsthand—and others I've observed and studied throughout the years—and provides a forum for church leaders and members to reflect on their own fishing ministries. At the end of each chapter and section of the book, I provide questions and activities to further guide you in fishing. I encourage you to honestly assess your church and yourself as you set out on this mission. It will only aid you in becoming more attractive to the fish you're trying to catch—so they too may become a part of God's family through Christ.

Part 1 – Getting Fish To Your Church

What is Evangelism?

One of the greatest disservices the modern church has done to evangelism is to create the official title "Evangelist." Unfortunately, the existence of this title implies that the duty and responsibility of evangelism resides with only certain individuals within our church. It becomes easy to let ourselves off the hook (no pun intended) by simply saying "I am not an evangelist." Well, the truth is… you are an evangelist. Every believer is called to spread the good news of Jesus the Christ and invite others into his fellowship.

He said to them, "Go into all the world and preach the gospel to all creation." (Mark 16:15, NIV)

When Jesus called the first disciples in Luke 5, he said to Simon, "Don't be afraid; from now on you will fish for people."(Luke 5:10b, NIV)

To be a disciple means "fishing for people." This is not an assignment that resides with a few; this is an assignment that resides with all. We are all fishermen and fisherwomen, and the fish are the people in the world swimming through the murky waters of life yet to discover the wonderful love of Christ. There are plenty of fish and yes, they are biting! The harvest is ripe and bountiful, but the laborers are few and far between. Are you ready to catch some fish? Get ready to be fishers of all people. You are called to be an evangelist, one who points others to the saving grace of Christ.

But where exactly are you pointing these fish? Start off by looking at the conditions of your church—the place you are trying to invite fish into, the place you want them to feel welcomed and comfortable so they can hear the good news of Christ. How much time do you—the church-- really spend thinking about the people you are trying to attract to your environment, the people you want to take the bait and reel in so they can develop and nurture relationships with Christ? How much of your programming is geared toward getting fish in the sea to attend your church?

Or, be honest, is your church more satisfied with feeding the fish already in the bowl who already belong to its flock? Is your church a gathering place for the saints of God who already know God's love? Is it only a refueling station for your members so they can get through the crazy and hectic week? While these are important functions of the church—and necessary—I know they are not the only function of the church. In fact, Jesus himself said: "It is not the healthy who not need a doctor, but the sick." (Matthew 9:12) And yes, your congregation needs to be continually fed and nurtured, and of course refueled for the week, but it is dangerous to get too comfortable with serving only those who are healthy—or those who know the love of Christ. One way we grow is to do the work of the Lord, which is evangelism, the catching of other fish.

Do you think evangelism is your job? Do you think creating an environment ripe for the fish is as important—or more important—than having a holy ghost-filled, spiritually uplifting church experience Sunday after Sunday?

It can be a tough question to consider. Seeing our primary role as being fishermen means we momentarily take the focus off of ourselves—and our spiritual needs—and refocus them on the fish outside of our church. We truly begin to look at the conditions of the water and meet the needs of those swimming around lost outside of our sanctuary doors. It's our calling. It's our mandate. It's what Jesus meant when he said he was calling his disciples to be fishers of people.

Are you ready to go fishing? Are you ready to show the fish your Christ and the saving and amazing grace a relationship with Jesus brings? Are you ready to make your church attractive to fish so they might be drawn to your Savior? It's time to go fishing.

Reflect on your personal attitude toward evangelism.

How often do you invite a family member or friend to your church?

How often do you invite a person you do not know well to church?

What keeps you from inviting people more often?

Reflect on your church's attitude toward evangelism.

On average, how many visitors come to your church each week?

How many visitors return to your church after the first week?

How welcoming do you think your church feels to a visitor?

Fish Habits

Most churches don't realize how self-centered they really are. I know that may come across as a harsh statement, but it can be true. When I say think like a fish, I really mean to let the habits, behaviors and ideas of the fish guide the process, even when they contradict your own conveniences, understandings, and traditions. It means seeing church through the eyes of the non-believing, unchurched, inexperienced fish.

For example, most fishing takes place early in the morning. There is nothing convenient about getting up at 4 a.m. and driving by a bait shop and out to a lake at the crack of dawn. However, if I am going to catch fish, then I must understand that this is the best time to catch fish. The habits of the fish determine the process. The fisherman is the one who adjusts to the habits of the fish, not the other way around. Why? Because it is the fisherman's sole intention to catch as many fish as he can that day. Therefore, the fisherman thinks like a fish and goes out early when the fish are hungriest and awaiting the bait.

I once asked my church what time should Sunday Morning Worship Service start. People said 10 a.m. because they like being home by Noon. Some said 11 a.m. because they like to sleep in on Sundays. Others said 8 a.m. because an early service allows them to get worship out of the way and enjoy the rest of their day. But, a true evangelist—one concerned about the fish floundering about in the worldly sea—would turn that question around and ask: "What time do the fish bite?"

When we think like fish, our worship times aren't driven by our own conveniences but by the habits of the fish. That's thinking like a fish. If we are posturing ourselves to reach professionals who tend to normally get up early, maybe 8 a.m. is best. If our fish are young people who tend to stay up late on weekends, maybe 1 p.m. is best. There is no right or wrong answers or times here; the real issue is for the church to remember that it's not about us, but it's about the fish. Jesus came for the sick, not the healthy (or those who have received his medicine already). Jesus wants a relationship with those who do not know him.

So, in addition to the time of your services and programs, what other things do you need to consider while preparing to fish? Fishermen know the waters; they know when they are cold and when they are warm. They know what temperature produces more fish looking for bait. Sometimes similarly, circumstances around a community or a group of people can force them to want to try something new or different. Bait, in essence, is food and nourishment. It's something the fish is looking for and needing right now. Your church services and worship services should be bait, something nurturing and attractive that the fish need and desire.

But how will the fish know about your church? About your Jesus even? How will they know to come close to your bait and sniff it out to see if it is something they want to try? Your message to the outside world, the fish, is critical.

So, start by studying the waters of those around you and those you want to attract. What do they need? Who are they? What do they like to do? What are the circumstances pressing in on their lives now? What do they read or watch or listen to? How will your bait lure them over?

Reflect on your community.

What are the main needs of those who live within 10 blocks of your church?

How many people within those 10 blocks attend your church?

What service or services does your church provide to attract the community?

What service or services do you think your church should provide to attract the community?

Brand Your Church

In order for the fish to bite, they must see—and be attracted to—the bait. Likewise, it is important that your church be visible in the community and visible in today's digital community. Like any other business, you must market and promote your church.

Branding your church is important. This includes a logo, a consistent color scheme and look or feel that resonates throughout your visible presentations and conveys the philosophy and priorities of the church. It need not be complex, and it shouldn't be. Good branding will be simple, bold and hard to forget. You want every business card, letterhead, envelope, web page, visitor card, etc. matching. This will strengthen your marketing and present you in a professional manner, thus telling people you are serious about what you are doing.

Every church needs a website. This is the first place people will go to learn more about your organization. It is your church's digital resume. Your website should be clean and inviting, not cluttered and difficult to navigate. Make sure the most important information is on the home page and is found easily. Unfortunately, many web surfers may only go this far. Important information includes your church's address, the time services start and something explicitly saying people are welcomed here. Photos will also be important. Images should not only reflect the make-up of your congregation, but also the desired makeup of your congregation (think ethnicity, age, etc). Images should be bright and faces should be smiling and welcoming.

Reflect on your church's website.

Does your church have a website?

Do you think the website is inviting?

If your church has a website, go to the site now and answer these questions: What do your images on your site say about your church?

Is the information on your site accurate and up to date?

Is there a way to contact the church through your website?

More Branding

If your budget allows, make sure you have a large and visible sign in front of the church building. This will tell those in the community that something is happening. It will also prove to be a valuable tool in articulating information regarding community and neighborhood events. And check the placement of this sign. Is it positioned in a place that you see only after you've turned into your church? You want people to see your church's sign before they turn into your church. Your sign should point fish to your church before they arrive—or know they want to visit.

Printed literature is a must. Whenever you meet someone or run into someone or have a visitor at your church, you need to be able to hand them something to take home. Equip members with invite cards or flyers as well. I have been in many situations where I ran out of business cards and a member had a few invite cards in his pocket or her purse. What a wonderful feeling!

You should also consider the powerful use of social media to attract those in the digital age. What is being posted on Facebook? Do you tweet about your church? Do you send out devotions that others forward (with your church's name attached, of course). Fish of today are infiltrated with information via social media. Even if you do not use it, you need to have someone in your church who is proficient post messages for you—this is a perfect place to engage young people who seem to have been born holding smart phones. Social media is second nature to young people and a wonderful way to encourage them to use their skills to reach fish.

When I arrived at my church I immediately recognized the lack of Social Media presence, so I set out to recruit what I would call the Social Media Ministry. I simply asked the congregation, "Who is on Facebook every day?" Three young ladies raised their hands. I then pulled out my phone and said, "If I message you right now, would you get an alert immediately?" One girl said yes. This meant she had her notifications turned on and thus steadily interacted with Facebook. I spoke with her and asked her to post news, pics and scriptures or devotions weekly, and she agreed. I shared with her a few web resources to draw scriptures and devotionals from and she was on her way. Later we adopted a social media management system (such as HootSuite) that allows a single post to hit multiple streams including

Instagram and Twitter. Social Media ministry accomplished and one more young person playing an active role in the fishing process. Done!

And while I'm talking about young people, I want to add that I personally think it is okay to allow your young recruiters to use their own language when recruiting for your church. While your grammar teacher may cringe, know that there is a correct way to use slang and language that attracts younger fish. Try to think of it as bait—something that will get the attention of the fish. And, your ultimate goal is to guide that fish into your boat and introduce him or her to the love of Christ—I can risk using slang for that!

Church branding means I have a presence and I want to remind you that I am here, where I'm at, how to get to me, and the times you can get to me—which should be very easy to find on your church's website, social media pages and any literature you hand out.

Reflect on your church's branding

Gather every piece of literature you provide about your church. Look through each piece and complete the checklist.

Item _____
Is your church's address included? Yes   No
Are service times printed? Yes   No
Is the church's website listed? Yes   No
Is the church's phone number printed? Yes   No

Item _____
Is your church's address included? Yes   No
Are service times printed? Yes   No
Is the church's website listed? Yes   No
Is the church's phone number printed? Yes   No

Item _____
Is your church's address included? Yes   No
Are service times printed? Yes   No
Is the church's website listed? Yes   No
Is the church's phone number printed? Yes   No

Item _____
Is your church's address included? Yes   No
Are service times printed? Yes   No
Is the church's website listed? Yes   No
Is the church's phone number printed? Yes   No

Item _____
Is your church's address included? Yes   No
Are service times printed? Yes   No
Is the church's website listed? Yes   No
Is the church's phone number printed? Yes   No

Go Where the Fish Are

I have fished with many of friends and families and anytime someone says we are going fishing, they mean that they are going to a body of water. It's simple. To fish, you have to go where the fish are.

Remember Matthew 9:11-12: When the Pharisees saw this, they asked his disciples, "Why does your teacher eat with tax collectors and sinners?" On hearing this, Jesus said, "It is not the healthy who need a doctor, but the sick."

You cannot catch fish if you are not among the fish. Many believers will be more concerned about what someone says or thinks when they are frequenting certain crowds because, unfortunately, people assume that birds of a feather always flock together. You must move beyond this if you are going to reach the fish.

One of our church's annual events was a car show. It was a great time with food, a disc jockey and even line dancing in the parking lot. It was also a fundraiser. We used this event to finance the laptop computers we would give to graduating seniors who decided to pursue higher education. I knew that an effective car show needed plenty of cars, and I knew where to find them. I had already contacted the Old School Car Clubs and others, but the cars I really wanted were in the hood, at midnight, on the weekend, at the liquor store. The liquor store was attached to a nightclub and it was a very popular place on the weekends. I knew it was risky and borderline unsafe, but I was determined to evangelize the young people and get them (and their cars) to our car show. After a few nights, security knew me by name, and the owner had no problem with me being at the door. What was amazing was how many young people came and participated in the car show. What was even more amazing was the backlash I received from church members. What is the pastor doing at the liquor store? Needless to say, the car show was a huge success and became a community event. I could not get many of those people to church for worship, but I did get them in the parking lot and among the believers. And no doubt, when the conditions in their lives prompted them to want to attend a worship service, they would remember our church. The fish now knew where our church was.

I must pause here to say; BE SAFE! I did have the advantage of being known in the community so I anticipated a few people would recognize me as a Pastor. You must be conscious of where you are and who you are with. Unfortunately, your Christian message will not be welcomed everywhere and some places you just should not be going for the sake of your physical well-being. Taking a few people with you is a must. Wear matching T-shirts or badges as a visible indicator as to why you are there. And keep your focus on getting to the fish; your job is to get fish to know about your church and a service you provide.

Reflect on your willingness to go where the fish are.

Where is the most radical place you or your church has handed out flyers about an event at your church?

Think of a place you have not ventured before where fish gather. How beneficial do you think it would be for people there to know about an upcoming church service or program?

Develop a plan to show up at this new place and share information about your program (include seeking permission to distribute information at the location).

Language

Whether we are talking about a website, flyer or the sign out front, language is most important. The difficulty for most believers when it comes to thinking like a fish is that many of us have never been the fish. We grew up in church and church has always been a part of our lives, so we are very detached from the realities of a true new believer. This becomes most evident when we talk about language.

Think of your three favorite church sayings and/or scriptures. Inevitably you used words such as:

grace, redeemed, saved, sanctified, thou, shall, holy spirit, justified, works, Christ, heaven, angels, enemy, and blessings.

Simply put, these words are church jargon. For a person who has never been to church or knows very little about Christianity, these words mean nothing and you may as well be speaking a foreign language. We want to use words that convey simplistic messages and concepts that stand above and beyond ecclesiastical language. Talk about being loved, accepted and welcomed. Talk about the pains of life and the frustrations of your every day vicissitudes. Talk about family and laughter and the joy of coming together with like-minded people. These concepts reach beyond the walls of the church and are much easier for anyone to grasp.

Read Matthew 13:1-9

Why does Jesus choose a parable that talks about a farmer planting seeds? Jesus is evangelizing in an agrarian community. He was talking to farmers and country people so he uses the language they can relate to.

Read Ephesians 6:10-17

Why does Paul use military language to convey his message? Paul is evangelizing an urban community. He was talking to people who were familiar with government, politics and military presence. He uses the language they can relate to.

Who are you trying to reach and what is their language?

As much as possible, make sure every vehicle you use to invite others to Christ is written in verbiage that can be easily understand. We want to relate with people, not baffle and confuse them.

The Conversation

Related to the idea of language is the concept of conversation. As you talk to others about Christ and your church, conversation will ensue. It is my belief that many people don't evangelize because they are fearful of not being able to answer certain questions or they don't think they are adequately equipped with bible knowledge. I do understand. I have always said, "Competence breeds confidence." We are always confident in discussing the things we know best. We have no problem talking about our favorite recipe, soap operas, sports teams and such because, again, we have no problem talking about the things we know well.

It is important for you to know that evangelizing is not about taking a boat load of scriptures and sharing them with people. To the contrary, I think this is completely the wrong approach. First, we have a language issue (as discussed before) and secondly, this assumes that others, particularly fish, see the bible in the same authoritative manner that you do.

Remember, the bible is a great story, but it is not your story. It is the story of the Hebrew people and written at a time when none of us were on earth. I would like to suggest that a much more effective tool is telling your own story.

First, your conviction will always be strongest when telling your own story-- because you have lived it. And because you have lived it, it is very hard for someone to convince you of anything other than what you have experienced for yourself.

Secondly, your own story will be contemporary and does not contain the church jargon that often baffles and confuses non-believers.

Finally, people can resonate with your story because you are standing there to share it. They do not see Jonah, David or Samuel. They can, however, see you.

People want to know the difference God has made in YOUR life. Why do you spend your valuable time and resources going to church? Tell them how God helped you at your most troubled time. Tell them how God provided for you when you least expected it. Tell them how you were loved back to life by a community of great people. Now you are telling stories people can relate to and you are sharing a benefit that is appealing. The beauty of this approach is that it is not only heart-felt and real, but it requires no scripture knowledge. You will also find that religious arguments will be far and few because you are not discussing religion per se. You are discussing your life. The life you know and have lived for yourself. Simply put, people want to know "what has God done for you?"

Reflect on your testimony.

Stop now and think about how you came to Christ? What were the events surrounding your decision to accept Christ?

What recent ways have you seen God move in your life?

Share your testimony with a church member now; it will give you practice when approaching fish.

More Will Say No Than Yes

Remember the Parable of the Sower we read earlier: Matthew 13:1-9. Let's do a little math. Jesus says that only one of the four seeds lands on good soil. That is a 25 percent success rate and a 75 percent fail rate.

Evangelism can be frustrating because we want everyone we talk with to buy in. Unfortunately, that will not be the case. This parable reminds us that more people will actually say no than yes. When we set out to evangelize, we must mentally prepare ourselves for people to say no, and say it more often than yes. No does not mean that you have failed or that you did something wrong. It's just a reality. Many will say no.

Evangelizing is not about persuading people to come to Christ or the church immediately per se. It is about seed planting. Some seeds will germinate immediately, people will be excited and ready to apprehend what you have to offer. Other seeds may take time. You may invite someone to church and they say no, but that does not mean that your time was wasted. They may go home, think about it a while and show up later (this is why the literature is important). They may forget about it for years until something happens in their lives and they recall the conversation you had some time ago. What I am saying is a "no" is not a failure. You are planting seeds, and when we see it as such, it is much easier to endure the feeling of rejection that can often accompany evangelism. Just keep planting seeds and something is bound to grow!

Think about a good fisherman. Does he stop when he gets no fish or does he adjust his perspective and position? Now, he might pack up one day and go home with a big catch, but if he is a serious fishermen, he will no doubt be back on the water bright and early the next morning. Your congregation needs to have the same attitude about evangelizing. Don't focus on the ones you're not catching; rejoice and be glad with the ones you are catching—and learn to adjust your perspective and position so you can catch others.

Reflect on Rejection

How do you feel knowing that 25 percent (or less) will say yes to your invitation to come to your church?

How can you prepare yourself to keep going in the face of rejection?

How do you see persistence and determination in relationship to evangelizing?

The Presentation

If you haven't figured it out yet, a lot of the *Think Like A Fish* concept is not about the message, but more about the presentation. Often, we can have the right message or the right bait, but if we are not careful in considering language and context, we will be ineffective because of our presentation. We want to present a gospel that is attractive, simple and appealing. We want a presentation that invites inquiry and further investigation.

A good friend, Pastor James Moody, shares a wonderful story about a fishing trip he took with his father. They were fishing with small rubber tadpoles (baby frogs) as bait. Pastor Moody was throwing his bait in the water then reeling it in, then throwing it in the water, then reeling it in. He could not figure out why he was so unsuccessful even though he was using the same bait as his father. His father explained that while the bait was in the water it was not enough to just reel it in. Instead, you have to tug and wait, tug and wait, tug and wait. James' father explained that this method makes the tadpole look like it is actually swimming and thus makes it look realistic and more appealing to the fish. So my friend had the right bait, just the wrong presentation.

If we are going to get individuals to our church, we must be conscious of every aspect of our presentation, from language to format and location. It is no good posting flyers at the High School for your next Seniors Ministry meeting. It is no good creating literature that is scripture filled and then handing it to non-believers. It is no good having a website full of information, but it is so convoluted that a fish can't find the information he or she needs to show up at your church. It's about presentation. It's not just *what* we share, but *how* we share it.

Reflect on fishing.

How many times do you share printed information (flyers, bulletins, etc.) with others who do not attend your church?

How comfortable do you feel sharing your church's current printed information with others?

What improvements would you make to your church's printed material? Is there any type of material you'd like to have that you don't currently have?

How do you think your testimony can draw others to Christ?

How often do you share a testimony with others?

What keeps you from sharing your testimony?

Part 2 - Fish At The Church

Be A Fish

Close your eyes and try your best to think like a fish—a person who has never stepped foot into your building for worship service. Do you know where to park your car if you drive to service? Do you know which door to enter? Do you know whether to turn left or right when you enter that door? What about where to sit? Where are the restrooms located? What if you have a child or baby? Is there a place to change his or her diaper or get a snack?

And those are just questions about entering the church—we haven't even talked about whether to stand, sit, kneel, etc. But you should get the idea that your church can seem like a foreign land to a fish, especially one entering the church alone for the first time.

There is an increasing number of people in our world and community who are known as the "unchurched." I would like to emphasize that this term doesn't just mean that these people do not have a church home or are not listed in the roll book of a local church. This term "unchurched" can also mean that people have never seen the inside four walls of a sanctuary—ever.

These are the people who didn't attend church and Sunday school with their parents or grandparents. These are people who never went to Vacation Bible School with a neighbor or a friend. These are people who have never sat in a Bible class or a worship service—ever in life.

It can be difficult to understand how a person who doesn't even know what a church looks like inside feels or thinks when entering a church for the first time. But, if this is the fish you're after, it is wise to think like that fish and make your congregation more aware of ways to make the fish feel welcomed.

Jesus was often ridiculed for eating with "regular" folks, or as Matthew puts it "sinners." Jesus communed with people who were not a part of the religious culture. Jesus hung out with, for a lack of a better term, the "unchurched." The sinners were not well versed in the law. They did not sit up and pretend to have philosophical debates. They were pretty regular, ordinary, probably working folks. Some were tax collectors, a job seen as undesirable; some were prostitutes.

But I love how Jesus talked about the people he ate with; he said that healthy people didn't need a doctor, the sick did. In other words, Jesus came to take care of the sick and to save the sinners. He was clear on his purpose and he knew where to find his patients.

Clearly, this verse doesn't mean that those of us in the church do not need help or even salvation, but it does show why Jesus mingled amongst the "unchurched." The verse can also give us an impetus for reaching the fish— and thinking like they do in order to attract them to our church.

So how do you help fish navigate around the unfamiliar known as your church? How do you help fish feel comfortable enough to want to come back to your church and learn more about this doctor named Jesus?

Reflect on a fish entering your church.

Go back to the exercise where you closed your eyes and walked into your church for the first time. At your next church function, do just that. Walk in your church blindly (as if you are entering for the first time). Then answer the questions.

Did you know which door to use?

It may seem silly to have a sign on your door telling people where to enter, but it could help a fish. And make sure the sign is clear and large—for fish who do not see well (or perhaps may not read well).

Who is at the door greeting the fish?

Are greeters at your church trained to smile and extend a welcoming hand at everyone, not just the members they see each week.

How much time do greeters spend hugging known members versus asking a new fish if they need help?

Make Fish Feel Welcomed

One of the best examples of a welcoming greeters committee is the one I witnessed at St. Luke AME Church in East St. Louis, Illinois. The Men's Ministry served as the greeters. The day I visited the church, it was pouring down raining and the greeters went out to the curb side with large umbrellas and escorted members being dropped off into the church. It was amazing to see how surprised visitors were to receive this high level of hospitality. More importantly, this opening gesture set the proper tone for an enjoyable and memorable church experience.

Imagine what message that gives to a fish—especially if the fish was invited under the umbrella. Immediately, I would feel welcomed and safe and as if I'd be taken care of in this new, foreign place.

When thinking about welcoming fish, you also want to make sure your building has "welcoming" signs beyond the physical bulletin board or signage you use out front. Your church should welcome visitors through its appearance. A well-kept building and landscaping are important in letting people know you are alive and vibrant. Uncut grass and poor landscaping can easily be interpreted as an organization that is struggling or dying. Make sure trash is removed from around the building, particularly the entrance. If your parking lot has light bulbs, make sure they are lit and working.

Reflect on your church's building.

Walk around your church with new eyes. What do you observe?

What do you think your church building and grounds say to those who may be looking to come inside?

When The Fish Show Up

Whether it is a house or a huge building, there is always the challenge of finding your way around a place you have never been before, and church is no different. Entrances should be labeled clearly and it should be very evident which door is used for your main worship service(s). Greeters can be very instrumental in directing people who may be visiting for the first time.

Once I –a fish--have entered the building, does the signage direct me to the sanctuary and, just as importantly, the restrooms. One business that does this very well, at least sometimes, is hospitals. Hospitals are inevitably labyrinths and very difficult to navigate. Most hospitals provide signs to the elevators, restrooms, cafeteria, etc. and back to the main lobby. They even provide signs for the room number count once you are in the right wing. As a pastor, I have entered many hospitals for the first time and I can assure you, signs make life so much easier.

Don't assume your fish will find their way; help them out—it will make them feel more comfortable. One Sunday, my wife and I were visiting a church and they invited everyone for food in the Baber Hall after service. Of course, this name did not give us a clue as to what size room we were actually looking for, but we proceeded to find it nonetheless. As service dismissed people began to move in various directions, some were leaving and some were heading into the other areas of the building. The old trick of follow the crowd was not going to work. My wife leaned over to me and said, "wouldn't it be nice if greeters were still here after service directing people to the Baber Hall." Point taken. Don't forget your visitors—or fish—after service.

I have enjoyed wonderful growth during my ministry. I have had the unique privilege to pastor congregations of various sizes and even in another country. I have seen people of all ethnicities join our ministry from varying walks of life. I have often asked people, why did they join our church? I would ask them all, young, old, African-American, Caucasian, Hispanic, blue collar, white collar, Democrat and Republican. I would always get some variance of the same answer. They said: I felt loved and I felt welcomed. My ego wanted them to say the preaching or the music or something of that nature made them join. And while those parts of worship were very important in the decision to join our church, the main reason always came back to the same phrase— I felt loved, I felt welcomed.

Of course, we all would like to think our churches are loving and welcoming, but if we look at our growth—our retention of new fish—we have to take a realistic look at why people may not be joining us. Remember, we are talking about fish and fish do not come out of the water seasoned and ready for the plate. They come out stinky and gooey and covered with stuff. They have to go through a process before they are edible and the fish of the world are no different. Fish do not always know what is appropriate clothing, that food is not allowed in the sanctuary, when to stand and when to sit, when they can leave for the restroom and when it is most disturbing. This may come as a surprise, but you were not born knowing that stuff either. Someone or some experience taught you those things. There must be a level of tolerance in order to fish. There must be a reminder that everyone is not churched—and everyone is not accustomed to the things you take for granted Sunday after Sunday. More importantly, when a fish senses that they are "out of order" or will be judged for moving when others are not, they will recoil—and feel less welcomed, which no doubt impacts their decision to return and fully grasp your invitation to see Jesus.

I always cringe when I hear members critique someone's clothing on Sunday morning. If I have never been to church, my only idea of a dress or outfit may be the same as the one I wear to the night club, and depending on my resources, it may be the only one I own. So here I am, putting my best foot forward based on what I have and I walk in church and someone tells me there is something wrong with what I am wearing. Ugh! Not a good way to catch a fish. And you may not say these words out loud—many of us do have tact, but your glance and perhaps whispers can convey a louder message. Be careful with fish. Your goal is to reel them in to hear about Jesus—that's much more important than protocol at this point!

Remember, love acknowledges before it criticizes. Once people know you love them and the things you say are coming from a place of love then they are more ready to receive your commentary. Do not tell me what to wear and what not to wear and you do not even know my name, let alone, my circumstance or situation!

Fish do not know the church seating chart. To ask someone to move simply because you normally sit there is plainly ludicrous. It quickly sends a message of: I am somebody and you are not. The irony I always find is how did the visitor arrive before the regular member anyway, hmmm?! And I understand that you feel comfortable sitting in the seat you always sit in, but just for a moment, recall the point of your service—it's more than your getting your weekly worship fix on—it's about drawing others to your Christ. Would you really want your attitude—or glance or words-- about your regular seat to turn away a fish?

I hope you are seeing my point. Fish must be interacted with patience, delicateness and lots of love and kindness. We want people to know that God loves you as you are and we want to display that in our own behavior. The greatest way to show someone you love them is to take the time to get to know them.

Our church had grown like wildfire one year and many of my officers said in a meeting, "we appreciate all of the people, but we feel like we are sitting among strangers; we don't even know who they are." I laughed so hard that is was probably inappropriate. All I could say was "and whose fault is that?"

Many churches have a fellowship time where people hug each other and greet each other, sometimes called "passing the peace." I added a little twist. I asked everyone to try to identify someone they do not know, get their name, greet them and get back to their seat. We want everyone to know at least one new person before they leave; after all, who in their right mind would allow someone to come into their house and not take the time to find out who they are? Some things are so obvious we miss them.

And imagine how the fish would feel if you personally went over and greeted them the next time you saw them in service—rather than catching up with the member who sits by you every Sunday (and who you already know and can call on the phone anytime to really catch up!). If I were new to a church, having someone—even just one person—remember my name and remember that I was new would make me feel much more comfortable and would increase my chances of returning—and maybe even meeting Jesus and his unconditional love. It is important that you foster a spirit of love and welcome-ness in your church or organization or nothing else discussed in this book will work. Love is that important.

Reflect on visitors.

This week, take a look around and see how visitors are treated at your service.

How do members extend warmth to visitors?

Do members extend warmth before and after the welcome?

Do the signs in your church show how to get to the restroom?

Do signs in your church show where your fellowship hall or other gathering place is located?

What can you do to make visitors feel more welcomed?

It's time we look out for the fish we are trying to catch. Your kindness and warmth will be bait.

Using Feedback To Grow Your Church

Feedback is essential for businesses. They use the comments from customers to evaluate the company's performance. What areas do they need to improve? What areas are appreciated the most by customers? Yes, companies need to know the good just as much as they need to know the bad and ugly, because a company best not change the thing that really makes customers happy! But what about churches? How do we get feedback and truly make evaluations? A comment heard in passing in the parking lot—or a complaint from Sister Johnson through Brother Brown, who heard it from Mother Moore (you get the point—there's really no direct link for feedback in most churches).

Now, go one step further: do fish have a chance to provide you with feedback? After all, we've already established that one of our primary goals as a church is to attract fish and invite them to see Christ. But, if we have no idea how fish feel when they come to our church, how in the world will we make the needed changes—and keep enhancing what is attractive?

We need clear, concise, unadulterated feedback--real feedback. We need a real system to track comments from fish who enter our services. And let me be transparent here, the best feedback will not be glorious praises—those comments might make you feel good, but they will not give you a true picture of what fish see. You want to know the real deal and hear about the experience the new person had/has at your church. How else will you know what areas you and your members need to work on? The best source of information is often a sad source—it could come from a fish who has decided to never set foot into your church again.

When I initially recognized my church's need for feedback, I turned to the visitors' cards. However, I quickly found out that these cards were not the best source. For whatever reason, most people were not filling out the visitors' cards. And the few cards we did receive rarely offered insight into the visitor's experience.

So, I began to ask other pastors what they were using to gather feedback from visitors, and I found that most pastors didn't have an answer. So, my techie side kicked in (an answered prayer from God, helping to merge my dual personalities of pastor theologian and tech geek Jedi) and I called a friend of mine, a web developer. Together, my friend and I developed

PewHub (www.pewhub.com), a way for fish to share what swimming in your water is really like.

PewHub is a free online tool that allows visitors and members to provide real time feedback about their experience at your church. PewHub is designed to improve the quality of worship everywhere. PewHub is the intersection of client feedback and church organizations throughout the United States. It gives quality feedback mechanisms and advanced search options to the religious community and those seeking places of worship.

Quality Feedback Mechanisms

Quality customer feedback is essential to the vitality of any organization. How essential?

"Surveying your customers regularly and in a variety of ways is a critical part of running a successful business, regardless of your industry, product or service." - Huffington Post, 2012.

"You can consistently improve your products or services, and keep them being the best they can be. If you're consistently listening and seeking feedback, you always have a pulse on what's working for your customers and what's not." - Forbes Magazine, 2011.

"If you want a true assessment of how your company is doing, ask the next customer that walks through your door or calls you on the phone." - Entrepreneur Magazine, 2015

"Whether you are working with new or established clients, client feedback is critical to identifying what each client actually values. With that knowledge, you can provide the kind of service that will set you apart from the crowd…" - American Bar Association, 2012

PewHub invites members and visitors to participate in a brief, yet informative process that provides churches with more than just a simple comment at the door. Our unique rating system was developed by pastors and religious leaders to reflect those areas most important to church growth and development.

Simply put: this tool gives you direct feedback from the fish. Most people find it arduous to complete cards and write comments, however, as we know, people will type on their phones forever. PewHub allows members and visitors to rate their worship experience and share any comments or concerns right on their mobile devices. This information is then retained and compiled into reports that are e-mailed directly to church leaders. PewHub helps show you the strengths and weaknesses of your ministry. You will also receive comparatives quarterly showing how other ministries in your area rated. Advanced options allow you to respond to those reviews that may be less favorable and invite them for another look.

Now we are fishing! Instead of giving the fish what we think they want, PewHub gives the fish a chance to share what they are looking for and what they actually observed and experienced.

Reflect on your church's source of feedback.

How many completed visitors' cards do you receive each week?

How helpful do you think the feedback/comments you receive are?

Who receives and reads the cards?

Do you think it would be helpful to have more feedback from visitors about their experience at your church?

How do you envision using more feedback from visitors?

Part 3 – Getting Fish In The Church

Reeling the Fish

Well let's move now to what happens when you get a live fish on the line! The fish has taken the bait, attended one of your worship services or programs that attracted this particular fish, was welcomed into the service, posted a positive review on PewHub and felt compelled to come back. Now, that fish has taken the big leap and is ready to become a member of your church. Hallelujah! This is the moment you've been waiting for.

Let's remember the parable Jesus tells about the lost sheep and the lost coin in Luke 15 (and the lost son later in the chapter). Read the passage and look for the joy and excitement—it's found in the discovery—or rediscovery—of what was lost. We, as fishermen and fisherwomen, should rejoice with as much enthusiasm and joy as the shepherd, the woman, and the father. Have you ever seen a fisherman take a picture with his big catch? He's grinning from ear to ear, proud of what has been accomplished. I love churches that have walls that post pictures of their new members. Like good fishermen, they are sharing the beauty of their catch.

Our job is to bring in the lost and show them Christ. We are called to be lights in the darkness—and when someone makes a decision to walk into the light—by joining a church and connecting with the Jesus we preach-- we should be exceedingly joyful and glad. Does your congregation reflect the same joy when a fish makes the decision to walk down the aisle and connect with your church and your God?

Reflect on your church's welcoming process for new members.

Who meets new fish as they make the long walk down your aisle?

Who takes their information?

Who follows up with them?

Do you have new members' classes or orientation?

Do the teachers of those new members' classes embody the warmth of your church? Do they have the patience and mindset to deal with new people, new fish who may be swimming in a new place now?

Do you include a tour of your church for new members?

Making Room For New Fish

In addition to celebrating the step the fish has taken with joy and patience, does your congregation make room for the fish? This is what I mean when I say: getting them *in* the church. This is not always an easy task for seasoned saints—or members who have a strong connection to their church and to familiarity. Encourage members to constantly expand their minds and open their arms to all members, especially the new fish.

You may have to remind older members that new fish are just that—new. You don't expect them to act like old members who know all the rules—and follow all of them.

Fish can be much like little kids learning new boundaries and skills. When my son was 3 years old, he was eager, inquisitive and full of energy, like most 3 year-olds. One morning, this 3-year-old decided to try out his independence. He made up in his mind that he was going to make his own bowl of cereal without the help of Mom or Dad. We knew something was going on because it was very quiet, an unusual trait for a 3-year-old. We walked around to find him and sure enough, he was in the kitchen, sitting on the floor, in a puddle of spilled milk that apparently had fallen from the top shelf. To this day, I have no idea how he reached the milk other than possibly climbing on the door.

But as I looked at the huge puddle, I had a choice to make. I could be upset because I had 2% milk flowing like the rivers of the Nile across my kitchen floor or I could be encouraging because he took a step towards the independence that we readily promote in our children. I chose the latter.

New members don't know all of the rules, when to stand, when to sit, when to bow, when to put their left foot in and take their right foot out... I think you get the picture. For lack of a better term, new members can make a real mess. However, they have also done something courageous; they have shown up. I am suggesting that we celebrate their presence and overlook their mistakes. They will learn the do's and don'ts over time, as we all did.

By the time my son was twelve years old he was cooking roast beef, potatoes and carrots (true story) and loves to cook to this day. Imagine how many wonderful meals we would have missed had we discouraged his presence in the kitchen simply because he didn't get it right the first time.

Fishing takes patience, and remember just as fish come out of the water gooey and icky, some of our fish will too; but no worries, I promise they will clean up just fine. After all, you did.

One of my favorite examples of making room occurred at a church I pastored several years ago. We were planning a church picnic and choosing committee members. The committees were pretty standard as were as their duties. There was however, one difference, we had been growing so we had a lot more fish. In this particular meeting, a young lady who was in charge of the praise dancers (a small group of young girls) asked if the praise dancers could help on the serving line. Unfortunately, the response they received was not unusual. "We already have a routine going and we don't need them slowing us down." I was shocked. I knew how much courage it had taken the young lady to stand up and ask to be a part of this group and now she was being shot down. Ugh! I spoke to the committee and assured them that getting new fish involved was much more important than a perfect pile of green beans, and if my side dishes touching on the same plate was the expense I had to pay to see some young girls involved, well... so be it. The veteran committee members agreed and were actually very polite about it. They were really a great group-- some of my best members-- who took their jobs seriously and always wanted to perform to the highest of standards. As well intentioned as they were, they did not recognize how their words sounded to the fish until I brought it to their attention.

Here comes the irony: on the day of the picnic, it was scorching hot. When the picnic was over, one lady came to me and said, "I am glad we had those girls to give us a break." When we get the fish active, it helps everyone involved and helps build our church. That's what fishing is all about.

Getting your new members to feel a part of the church is critical to retaining them. Giving them a job—a place and position where they feel like their contributions matter—is inevitable to helping them further develop their relationship with God. I like to call it: No unemployed Christian. There is always a job for a Christian to do.

I like to remind people that the benefit of involvement in the church is biblical. You work out your salvation in community. You cannot learn love in solidarity. You cannot learn forgiveness unless you have someone to forgive—now, run with that when someone is hurt by a church member and wants to leave! You learn behavior indicative of a Christian by being in relationship with first God through Christ and then with your brothers and sisters. And the only way you are in relationship with one another is to be involved, to work with one another. And no doubt, you will learn some things and gain some character when you work with church folk.

Go Fish Activity

At your next planned event or program, invite several newer members to participate in the planning. Encourage veteran members to make the new members feel included.

What will you need to do to make new members feel welcomed on the committee?

Why Volunteerism Is Important?

Volunteerism is important because it leverages the power of the labor force you already have, but it also acts as a net to hold fish you have already caught. Unfortunately, I have had to take over some dying churches in my ministry. As any Pastor would, I often sought out those who had left the church in hope of convincing them to return and help rebuild the ministry. Do you know who the most difficult people to get to come back and stay were? It was those who had been gone long enough that they had a new job or position at their new place of worship. Their allegiance to their position acted as an anchor and significantly decreased the chances of them leaving.

Throw Out An Anchor

Like any good workforce, you must match jobs with employees; in our case, you must match fish with opportunities to serve. We often assume that people who want to serve will simply show up and say I am ready to work. Uhhh…it doesn't quite work like that.

The first step is creating a culture of volunteerism. Our church slogan (and we have many) is "No Unemployed Christians." I talk it. I have preached on it (Romans 12) and I continue to ask my members on a regular basis, "Do you have a job?" I am not referring to a secular job, I am referring to a Kingdom job. You must constantly remind members that every job is important and every position is significant. Many would suggest the Pastor or Head Officer is more important than the Janitor or Custodian. I would suggest that it is difficult to grow a church with a disgusting bathroom. All positions work hand in hand. The best ministry on the inside will never be discovered if it is concealed behind a lawn of uncut grass and shabby landscape. Children are not asked *if* they want to get involved, they are asked which ministry will they join. You can dance, you can usher or you can sing. Do you hear the assumptive close? When you come into our church, people need to know that they are not being asked to help, they are expected to help using their spiritual gifts and talents for Kingdom Building.

Secondly, you must get the word out on how to get involved and make sure you have opportunities available for each and every person who may come, regardless of how much they may or may not bring to the table.

This is why I love the Greeters Ministry-- anyone can do it. This ministry requires no prior scripture knowledge and training is minimal. Simply a smile, a "good morning" and a helping spirit is all you need. I call the Greeters Ministry my catchall. If you cannot sing-- and ushering or cooking or teaching or what have you is not your cup of tea-- you can always be a greeter. And we can never have too many greeters.

I received the most pleasant surprise of my life one morning. Two young teenage boys greeted me at the door this particular Sunday. They had on their T-shirts and blue jeans and the latest basketball shoes, clearly not typical church attire for our congregation. They were handsome young men, to say the least, and they were very good at greeting. It was obviously evident that they were having a good time. I didn't care how they looked that day, I was just glad to see a few fish had found a place to serve. It did present one problem. That door attracted a lot of young high school girls for some reason and I just don't know why (LOL). It's a good day when we see our young people getting involved and having fun serving the Lord and feeling like church is a place they want to be—and are welcomed.

Finally, this is not as a much of a do as it is a be. There is a difference between a volunteer and an employee. There is a greater difference between a church volunteer and an employee. Simply put, you are paying an employee. If your volunteer is a giving member, they are paying you. Let that soak in a minute.

We are not here to hire and fire people. We are here to involve people and sometimes that means taking extra time to train them and help them in their work for Christ.

My male chorus had some men in it that were well in age, upwards of 80 and 90. One particular man stood on his cane the entire time he sang. He could not walk in with the choir, he had to be helped into the choir stand before service. He could not clap or rock with the choir because of his cane and he loved standing in the front row. Admittedly, it was somewhat of an eyesore to see an entire choir moving in sync with a lone individual standing still right in the middle up front. A few members said it was time for him to sit down. I disagreed. If he was asked to sit down, we would be taking away his last resort for serving on Sunday. This is the difference between a church and a company. In a company, he would have been fired or moved. He clearly was not doing as expected. In a church, we are patient and understand the need for people to be involved in Kingdom Building.

You may have noticed by now that good fish involvement requires some overlooking. Whether it's the aesthetics of a plate of food at the church picnic or the synchronized motion of the choir, our desire for perfection and excellence cannot become so great that it eclipses the true purpose of the church--catching fish and getting them involved in Kingdom building.

Volunteerism is not only encouraging everyone, but also making sure there is a place for everyone desiring to get involved. It is our mission to cultivate an environment that makes room for everyone and throws out an anchor, a reason to stay and grow at this church.

I visited a mega church. They had a packet they were handing out. In the packet was a grid of all of the volunteer needs of the church. They included the hourly commitment, the amount of scriptural knowledge needed and the contact person. It was one of the best visible examples I have seen to date of an effective way to share volunteer opportunities with the congregation. Many of us want people to be involved, but we must also make sure there is a clear path to involvement.

Reflect on your church's volunteer opportunities.

What percentage, do you think, of your members have volunteer jobs at your church (or ministries they work in)?

Why do you think more members do not volunteer at your church?

How does your church let people know what volunteer jobs are available and need to be done?

Does your church let people know upfront the time commitment needed for each volunteer position?

Does your church let people know upfront the amount of biblical knowledge or other requirements needed for volunteer jobs at the church?

Part 4 - Getting The Church Into The Fish

Now that you have reeled in your fish and have given them a job—and everyone else in your church a place, what is next? The next phase of discipleship—after you've gotten the fish to your church and gotten them engaged—is to get the church in them.

I can explain this best by sharing what happened when I finally got to cook the meat for my family's annual cookout. I was excited to finally have an opportunity to run the grill and serve up the best hamburgers in the state of Iowa. I threw the match on the coals and the fire went up. I was all set to place the meat on the grill and get things going. But to my surprise, my dad ran out and shouted: "what are you doing?" I told him: "I'm putting the hamburgers on the grill; it's time for this party to get started." My dad looked at me with as much surprise and said: "No, it's not time yet. You have to wait until the coals are glowing. You're trying to cook with coals in the fire, but that's not enough. You need to wait until the fire is in the coals." My father was teaching me that I couldn't rush to put the meat on the grill. If I put the meat on prematurely, it would never get done. I needed to wait until the coals were glowing, which would mean that they were hot and ready to perform as intended. Coals cook best when they are hot. They do their job best when they are hot and glowing. I needed to wait until those coals got fire inside of them.

Similarly, we often get excited when people come into the church and are excited to see our numbers grow. But let us not forget that our main objective is not just to get people in church, but to get the church *into* the people. As a pastor, I know that there is a lot of literature about moving people from membership to discipleship—and I've read much of it. But, I'd like to add a third phase to this process and I call it ownership. The church should help people move from being members (belonging) to being fishers (disciples) to moving into ownership. You'll recognize people who have taken ownership because they will treat every facet of the church as if it were their own. They will do something simply because it needs to be done, even in the absence of a title or position.

You know your members have the church in them when they are compelled to turn around and go out and fish. They want to share their new found joy with others and bring them into their church. You have the church in you when you get enough love inside of you to want to draw others in. You have something shut up in your bones and you need to get it out by sharing it with others.

You can see the church inside of you by your commitment level. You began to live out the concept that I am a part of the church and it is a part of me. Where I go, the church goes. Your walk with Christ has moved from being an activity to being a lifestyle. You've moved from doing to being. Just as the coals must become one with the fire; ultimately, you want the spirit of Christ and your spirit to become one. The spirit of Christ burns through each of us who have the church in us and it prompts change, commitment, ownership, and the desire for evangelism. Once that spirit becomes a part of us, we are compelled to return and catch more fish, just as Jesus did.

You begin to say: I want to share this with others; I want it to be the best it can be; I want to serve; I want to share love; I want to grow. The church is not a separate entity or a merely a place to go; the church is in me and I am in the church. Now, church is more than an activity reserved for Sunday mornings; church is more than a place I take my kids; it's more than a seat or a song or sermon or a service.

Remember Romans 12. In this chapter of Romans, Paul urges us to offer our bodies as a sacrifice. The idea is sanctity proceeds true service. The goal of fishing is to get them in and to get enough love of Christ in them that they take on the very same mission that attracted them in the first place. They have the same mission as Christ, because they have the same spirit of Christ. The fire burns within the coals—ready to live out its purpose.

Think about how squirrels act. In Iowa, squirrels are plentiful and they can teach us how true evangelism works. You see squirrels hang out on back porches, especially in rural Iowa. And once the squirrels know you are feeding them on your back porch, they return to your porch each day to eat more. But when they have eaten enough nuts, they don't stop there and sit and be full. They go out and get other squirrels to show them the source of the nourishment. One squirrel returns with four more—all to show his pals the new found source.

This is why we want to fish. Fisherman not only catch fish, but they find humans and make them into fishermen. They use bait to catch fish. And for the church, our love is our strongest bait. Your bait—your love-- has worked and you've gotten them engaged. Now, you can teach them and help them grow their relationship with Christ. They have moved from fish to now getting prepared to be fishermen themselves.

What is needed to prepare the fisherman? Before they can effectively go out and evangelize, they've got to fully engage with why they are fishing. They have to meet Jesus for themselves and understand the power he has to change lives and the power he has to bring abundant life to ordinary people. They need to know why they want to fish, why they want to draw others closer to get a taste of this God and all of the benefits that come along with being included in the boat.

Reflection

What fruit do you bear that shows you have a personal relationship with Jesus?

What fruit do those in your church bear that imitates their relationship with Jesus?

Why do you want to be fishermen—drawing others to your church?

What things might you need to change to attract more fish personally to your church—and ultimately to your Jesus?

Genuine Hospitality

So, how do we really get the church inside of our fish?

As you contemplate your church's role as fishermen, I'd like to conclude by reminding you to not only focus on growing your church—or getting more fish—but to dig deeper into thinking about the area of hospitality. It's not that hospitality will grow your church or automatically draw fish, it's that a lack thereof will definitely prevent your church from catching (and retaining) fish. There is nothing worse than coming into a church with great preaching, inspirational music and wonderful ministries, only to find a group of non-welcoming cantankerous people.

Genuine hospitality must reach all people and this is where most churches fall short. We have an easy time inviting those who most look like us, but we fail to recognize the others we encounter every day at the grocery store, the bank, the school and the gas station. Our church printed thousands of invite cards that we asked all the members to carry and hand out. When I asked my predominantly African-American church how many invite cards they had given to non-black people, the answer was few to none. This quick assessment led me to move our church in a new direction regarding hospitality.

When we look at the word "hospitality" it is important to know that one of its Latin root word is hostis, which means stranger, but it also means enemy, i.e. someone who is hostile. We are called to invite our friends and our so-called enemies. Hospitality has traditionally been defined as the welcoming of strangers, but the hostile part has generally been omitted. Hospitality can be a scary thing, particularly when dealing with people who don't look, think or smell like you do. Genuine hospitality must walk in the love of Christ that overcomes this fear and sees the greater need to take that love of Christ to all people; even the ones we don't care for and yes, even the ones who are hostile.

When we look at our churches, we must consider hospitality on three levels.
To The Church – How are we encouraging people to visit our church?
At The Church – How welcomed do people feel when they do visit our church?
In The Church – Once a part of the church, do people feel a true sense of belonging?

To The Church

When we talk about genuine hospitality and the ability to attract all people to our church, the first thing we must look at are the mediums that we use to reach into the community and attract people to our church.

I've mentioned this before, but it bears repeating. Where we advertise says a lot about who we are trying to attract. If the only place you position business cards and posters is the local High Schools, you inevitably will be drawing on a High School crowd. If you only place advertisements in Nursing Homes, you inevitably will draw on a senior crowd. It is important that we strategically advertise in places that can be seen by all walks of life. Some good places are grocery stores, shopping malls, libraries and other public places. These places generally enjoy a wide range of cultures as their constituents and thus expose your church to a wide range of people.

What our advertising looks like also says a lot. The first thing people look for when they enter a room is those who most closely resemble themselves. As an African-American, I generally, even subconsciously, walk into a room and immediately notice how many other African-American males there are. There is a general human tendency to look for ourselves in a crowd. This tendency also relates to advertising. Your church website should show images of all ages and all ethnicities if you are trying to attract all people. Likewise, your church brochure and any other print advertising should do the same. Our church had one white person when I arrived and no website. When we built our first website, I intentionally included images of Caucasians, Hispanics and Asians to show our concern for all. We now have more Caucasian people joining and a Hispanic family who recently joined as well. It's a start.

At The Church

First impressions are everything. This proverbial business saying also rings true with regard to hospitality. Mark Waltz, Pastor of Grace United Methodist Church in Granger, Indiana writes, "The first impression occurs before the service begins—before the reading of the Scripture, before a song is sung, before the message is spoken. First impressions happen in the parking lot, at the entry of your building, in the children's hallways, and in your lobby or narthex."

Our doctoral student group visited Quinn Chapel AME Church in the downtown Chicago area. It is a thriving predominantly black church located in a predominantly black neighborhood. One of our professors, a white lady, arrived a little late and asked a young black man which door she should go in. He walked her to the door, opened it for her and told her "welcome." She shared this story with us as she expressed how sincere this gesture felt. The typical person would have pointed at the door or instructed her to the door, but this person went the extra mile. Did I mention this was in the middle of a Chicago January snowstorm? This first impression meant a lot.

It is important that our members understand that hospitality starts in the parking lot with them. Too often hospitality is relegated to a committee of Greeters, Ushers or such and it is pushed off as their job. As people scurry across the parking lot they should be speaking to one another. They should ask those they recognize as visitors if they have been here before. This creates the welcoming atmosphere before you enter the building. Speaking of which door to enter, it is also important that guests be able to navigate the property easily. One of the challenges we have had at Allen Chapel is getting people to recognize which of the four entrances leads to the sanctuary. We are in the process of rectifying this. Greeters should not only greet people, but they should direct them to Sanctuary, coat racks and restroom when necessary. It is always a strange feeling to be in a foreign place and our job is to minimize that feeling as much as possible. There are also ways to make your worship experience hospitable. We recently experimented with digital media by sharing the liturgy and songs on a screen for all to see. The result was amazing. Guests commented on how much easier it was to follow the flow of the service and, as a bonus; I was surprised at how many long standing members said they never knew all the words to some of the liturgy. Remember, the idea is to make a person feel comfortable and at home. Eileen D. Crowley writes in her book Liturgical Art for a Media Culture, "For individual members of a congregation, the inclusion of media in worship can mean greater access to the worship experience itself. It can be a mark of hospitality." She also reminds to be conscious of the images that we are using. "Diversity in the imagery of peoples, places, genders, and ages should be a consistent goal of media ministry."

C. Michael Hawn, faculty at Perkins School of Theology, offers a four-tier understanding of worship. First, there is the culturally uniform worship. This assumes that the participants have a common background and way of viewing the world. Second, there is worship through cultural assimilation. "This practice assumes a dominant cultural perspective that will become the common currency for all participants..." Third is the culturally open worship. This type of worship will "display a spirit of receptivity toward the community's cultural diversity, even though the congregation has a distinct cultural majority group." Fourth is a cultural partnership. "A cultural partnership takes place when no clear majority dominates and culturally diverse members reflect on the surrounding neighborhood and work together in a shared Christian community." It is this fourth tier that is hardest to achieve, yet most ideal if our worship is to be truly hospitable.

I had the wonderful opportunity to share in worship with a reconciling United Methodist Church on the West Side of Chicago. As a pastor, it was a good reminder of what it felt like to be the guest. Because I am African-American, I was sincerely curious as to how welcoming the worship experience would be. I was greeted pleasantly at the door and welcomed by a number of people. This was a good start. They had a projector screen that helped me follow the service, this was a better start. Then came the straw that broke the camel's back. I saw on the program "Pass Me Not," a traditional African-American hymn, and I was a little excited. When the time came to sing the hymn, what happened was even more amazing. They did not use the traditional melody of the song; they actually sang the modern gospel remix to the song. Here I was, in a predominantly white reconciling United Methodist Church, and I was getting my praise on! As if that were not enough, we closed the service with a very traditional song of the Black Church, "I Thank You Jesus." I applaud this pastor because it was clear that their worship experience was constructed with a little something for everyone. This is what a cultural partnership looks like and it is genuine hospitality at its best!

If our worship experience is going to be a cultural partnership, then we must develop our programs with a high degree of intentionality when it comes to including others. Not only did I enjoy the songs of my tradition, but I also enjoyed the rock and revolution songs that I was being exposed to. Because there something in it that made me feel at home, I was in a better place to receive that which was new and foreign to me. In essence, in its totality, this combination made the worship feel not so foreign at all.

In the Church

So you have loved them in the parking lot, you have greeted them in the door, you have comforted them in the worship service and they have joined church—now what? This is where the true test of Genuine Hospitality lies. Dr. Kim, professor of Garrett Evangelical Theological Seminary, tells the story of a church that was renting its building to a Hispanic congregation. They were loved and welcomed with open arms, until it came to the trustee meetings. A sense of frustration set it when they were allowed to rent the building, but not be a part of the decision making process. The attitude, more plainly put, was "it's ok to drive on our road as long as you stay in your lane." When members join our church, I constantly remind them that we have no hierarchy built on seniority. I do this because many new people are not encouraged to take leadership positions in the church; they are told to stay in their lane. A genuinely hospitable church is one that encourages full participation of its members, new and old.

These new members are also a vital resource in assessing just how hospitable your church really is. Please read this closely…hospitality can never be critiqued by those extending it, only those receiving it. As an African-American I have met a number of great Christians who extended the utmost heart-felt hospitality and did not realize that some of what they were doing was offensive to my culture. It was not that they didn't care, they just didn't know.

It was a hot summer day as hundreds of people gathered in the park for our neighborhood ice cream social. The other prominent church in our neighborhood was a predominantly white Lutheran church with about 1,500 members. As their pastor called me to the stage, he closed by saying "I know him personally, he's a good boy." If you could have seen the look on my congregation's face. Apparently, someone explained this to him as I received a phone call apologizing the next day. I knew it was an act of ignorance, not malice, and I assured him I was ok. We laughed about it and have been fine ever since.

Do not assume that just because you love God and have the best of intentions that your hospitality may not have nuances that may be offensive to certain cultures and people. Our church has enjoyed a few white people joining in the last year. Our next step is to take them to lunch and ask them what we can do to be more hospitable to their culture. Again, hospitality is something that you have to work at. It requires strong strategic and intentional thought and planning. It is important that what we say with our mouths and hearts is echoed in what people experience.

As a final thought, I have considered asking some of my friends to attend our church as secret customer service assessors. Restaurants have been using this concept for years. This may be a way for us to recognize areas where change and growth is needed. Genuine hospitality is not a goal, it is a journey. It is a journey that requires time and patience. We live in an ever changing world and we must constantly assess how we are meeting the needs of the people around us. If you are serious about growing your church, genuine hospitality must be in place. They will know that you are his disciples (not by the preaching or singing but…) by the love you show one another.

Fish are watching to see how we share the love with one another; often times, we talk about how we interact with people outside of church, but rarely do we talk about how we interact with each other as an example to fish.

I had an officer who was argumentative and border line disrespectful. This officer served on a particular board. When I put a new fish, who had great gifts and skills, on the board with the argumentative member, I noticed that the fish (or new member) soon became argumentative and disrespectful. She had watched the other officer carry out the same inappropriate behavior in the same setting. That's when it dawned on me, new members take on the existing ethos of the church; if we talk to each other nastily in a meeting, they think that's how we are supposed to talk with each other. That's why it is important that we are sharing the love with each other that we expect the fish to share. We have to display among ourselves the very love we are trying to convey to others.

The first time I went to a fancy restaurant and saw these little bowls of lemon water, I was thinking this had to be the plainest soup ever—no color, no seasoning, etc. Luckily, I looked around and observed what others were doing. They were washing their hands. I soon joined in and washed mine too. I mimicked the behavior of those around me. And this is exactly how fish behave. They start acting and doing what others are doing. We want to make sure that they are mimicking the love of Christ. It's what we want them to see and mimic.

Notice, in John 13:35, Christ said, "everyone will know that you are my disciples if you love one another." I think Christ is saying the way we as disciples love each other shows others who we really are; our mark of distinction is our love for each other. Check the love in your church. Observe how you interact with each other. Surely your love (or lack thereof) is evident to outsiders like the fish. And when our love is evident for each other, fish will be attracted to this love and will eventually mimic it.

Loving one another and loving others (fish) will become the process by which we get the church in the people. By fostering an environment of love—like Christ's love—we get the spirit of Christ inside of each other. And we have the church inside of us. True love always permeates the spirit. Even if it takes a while, light always overcomes the dark. Patience and love reign.

So when fishing, remember to invite the fish in, create a place for them to volunteer and be loving and patient with them—and most importantly, show the love of Christ among ourselves. Unfortunately, sometimes we treat new people special until they are not new anymore. When they first come in, everyone is loving them and giving them special attention, but soon they can fall into the background. When we truly Think Like Fish and incorporate the evangelism in this book, we don't want to just love fish to get them into the church, we want to love them continuously and ongoing. The same joy we expressed when they first joined the church, should be the same joy we express when they roll up every Sunday

That's why I believe church social events are critical to the health of a church. The picnic—or other event—is where we share in an informal setting. We don't have the choir or the ushers or deacons—we just have people eating together and having fun. These events strengthen the family bond. Relationships are built through shared time and share experiences. Often times people overlook the importance of social events because they feel they are not directly related to faith; but, in my opinion, these events are just as important. In these settings, the love of Christ is strengthened. Most Jesus' recorded relationships were not nurtured in the synagogue but at the dinner table.

Jesus' love was so powerful that what began as him seeking out people transformed into people seeking out him. What a testimony when others are drawn to you and your church because what they experience through love becomes something they want to seek out. That's the real deal when fishing. It's like having a boat where the fish jump in before you even try to catch them. Your very presence serves as the bait—drawing people in—because the love of Christ is so strongly displayed that people come running, wanting to seek Him. We want our love to be so strong that it draws others, that people will seek to know Christ through us.

After all Jesus promised in John 12: "When I be lifted up, I'll draw all people unto me." How are people seeing Christ in you? Is your church lifting up the example of Christ's love high enough for others to see and to come running to meet Him? It's our mission. It's our purpose. It's life-changing work. Let's go fishing!

Reflect on your love for one another.

How often does your church host social events for members?

How often do you attend social events with your church family?

How would you evaluate the love shown to one another within your church?

Do you think fish see members of your church loving each other? Explain

Would the interaction between your members make you want to learn more about Christ if you were a fish looking in from the outside? Explain.

List five things you will do differently to attract more fish to your church.

List five things you think your church should do differently to attract more fish. Discuss with your group.

Additional Notes:

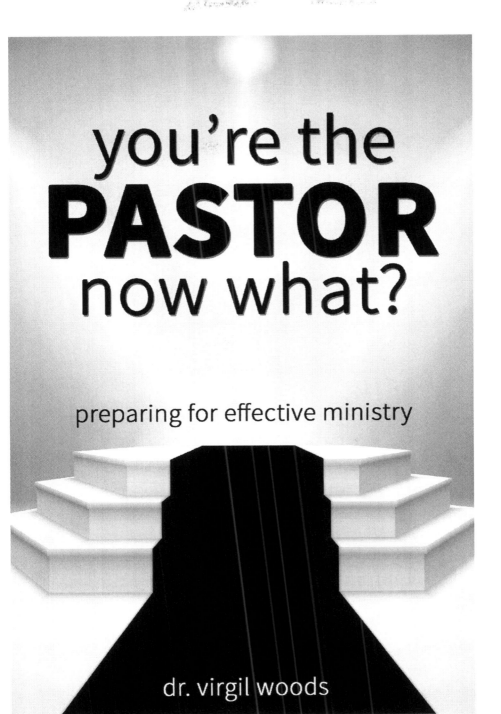

you're the PASTOR now what?

preparing for effective ministry

dr. virgil woods

Made in the USA
Lexington, KY
02 April 2018